The Upda

U.S. Citizenship Test

Workbook and Study Guide

2021-2022

128 Practice USCIS Questions

Jeffrey B. Harris M.Ed

The Updated U.S. Citizenship Test Workbook and Study Guide 2021-2022 : 128 Practice USCIS Questions

By Jeffrey B. Harris

Introduction

In order to become a citizen of the United States, there are four tests that you must pass:

1. Speaking Test

2. Reading test

3. Writing test

4. Civics test

Starting December 1st, 2020, there are **128** potential questions that will be asked on the civics portion of the naturalization test. **20** questions are asked, and you must answer **12** correctly. This book is set up to act as a study guide. The first half contains the questions and the second half contains the answers. You should write down the answer in the space provided once you truly know it. Also, new rules state that if you're over 65 years old and have lived in the United States for 20 years or more, then you only need to know the questions marked with a star. Good luck!

The questions throughout represent the actual questions found on the USCIS exam. Although, in this workbook there is variety in the style of questions (multiple choice, true or false, fill in the blank, short answer), and the real exam will be verbal and short answer.

Part I   Civics

Questions

<u>Multiple Choice</u>

1. What is the form of government of the United States?
    a.   Direct Democracy   b. Autocracy
    c.   Parliamentary Republic   d. Federal Republic

2. What is the supreme law of the land?*
    a.   Declaration of Independence   b. Amendment
    c.   The Constitution   d. Articles of Confederation

3. The U.S. Constitution does not
    a.   Explain the functions of Government
    b.   Protect the citizens of the US
    c.   Define the powers of government
    d.   Include any amendments

4. The U.S. Constitution starts with the words "We the People." "We the People" does not mean
    a.   The consent of the governed
    b.   Only the people born in America
    c.   Popular sovereignty
    d.   People should govern themselves

5. How are changes made to the U.S. Constitution?
    a.   Popular vote   b. Amendments
    c.   26 States vote   d. 51 votes in the Senate

6. Which answer best explains whom the Bill of Rights protect?
    a.   Rights of Americans   b. Rights of the President
    c.   Rights of Senators   d. Rights of those in power

7. How many amendments does the U.S. Constitution have?*
   a. 10   b. 23   c. 27   d. 19

8. What founding document said the American colonies were free from Britain?
   a. Declaration of Independence   b. Magna Carta
   c. Mayflower Compact   d. The Constitution

Short Answer

9. Why is the Declaration of Independence important?
_____

10. Name two important ideas from the Declaration of Independence and the U.S. Constitution.
_____
_____

11. The words "Life, Liberty, and the pursuit of Happiness" are in what founding document?
_____

12. What is the economic system of the United States?*
_____

13. What is the rule of law?
_____

True or False

14. Many documents influenced the U.S. Constitution, including the The Iroquois Great Law of Peace. _____
If false, write the correct answer_____

15. There are three branches of government because even numbers would be a tie. _____

If false, write the correct answer_____

16. One of the three branches of government is the Constitution. _____
If false, write the correct answer_____

17. The President of the United States is in charge of the Executive branch of government._____
If false, write the correct answer_____

18. The part of the federal government that writes laws is the Judicial Branch. _____
If false, write the correct answer_____

19. The two parts of the U.S. Congress are the House of Commons and the Senate. _____
If false, write the correct answer_____

20. One power of the Executive Branch is to enforce the law. _____
If false, write the correct answer_____

Fill in the blank

21. There are _____ U.S. senators.

22. A term for a U.S. senator lasts _____ years.

23. _____ is one of your state's U.S. senators now?

24. There are _____ voting members in the House of Representatives.

25. A term for a member of the House of Representatives is _____ years.

Short Answer

26. Why do U.S. representatives serve shorter terms than U.S. senators?

27. How many senators does each state have?

28. Why does each state have two senators?

29. Name your U.S. representative.

30. What is the name of the Speaker of the House of Representatives now?*

31. Who does a U.S. senator represent?

32. Who elects U.S. senators?

33. Who does a member of the House of Representatives represent?

True or False

34. The President elects members of the House of Representatives._____
 If false, write the correct answer_____

35. Some states have more representatives than other states because of higher populations. _____
 If false, write the correct answer_____

36. The President of the United States is elected for six years_____
   If false, write the correct answer_____

37. The President of the United States can serve only two terms so he/she doesn't get too powerful. _____
   If false, write the correct answer_____

38. Mike Pence is the name of the President of the United States now. _____
   If false, write the correct answer_____

39. Kamala Harris is the name of the Vice President of the United States now. _____
   If false, write the correct answer_____

Multiple Choice

40. If the president can no longer serve, who becomes president?
   a. Vice President b. Secretary of State
   c. Speaker of the House   d. Secretary of Defense

41. Which is not one power of the president.
   a. Sign laws   b. Enforce laws
   c. Chief diplomat d. Make laws

42. Who is Commander in Chief of the U.S. military?
   a. Secretary of Defense   b. President
   c. Vice President   d. Secretary of State

43. Who signs bills to become laws?
   a. Senators   b. Congressmen
   c. President   d. Vice President

44. Who vetoes bills?*
    a. Senators   b. Congressmen
    c. President   d. Vice President

45. Who appoints federal judges?
    a. Senators   b. Congressmen
    c. President   d. Vice President

46. The executive branch has many parts. Which is not one?
    a. President   b. Cabinet
    c. Senate   d. Federal Agencies

Short Answer

47. What does the President's Cabinet do?

48. What are two Cabinet-level positions?

49. Why is the Electoral College important?

50. What is one part of the judicial branch?

51. What does the judicial branch do?

52. What is the highest court in the United States?*

Multiple Choice

53. How many seats are on the Supreme Court?

a. 5   b. 9   c. 12   d. 15

54. How many Supreme Court justices are usually needed to decide a case?
    a. 5   b. 9   c. 12   d. 15

55. How long do Supreme Court justices serve?
    a. Three terms   b. Four terms
    c. Five Terms   d. For life

True or False

56. Supreme Court justices serve for life to limit political influence. _____
  If false, write the correct answer_____

57. The Chief Justice of the United States is Clarence Thomas. _____
If false, write the correct answer_____

58. Education policy is only for the federal government._____
  If false, write the correct answer_____

59. Printing money is only for the states._____
  If false, write the correct answer_____

60. The purpose of the 10th Amendment is freedom of speech. _____
  If false, write the correct answer_____

Fill in the Blank

61. _____ is the governor of your state now.

62. _____ is the capital of your state.

Short Answer

63. There are four amendments to the U.S. Constitution about who can vote. Describe one of them.

64. Who can vote in federal elections, run for federal office, and serve on a jury in the United States?

65. What are three rights of everyone living in the United States?

66. What do we show loyalty to when we say the Pledge of Allegiance?*

67. Name two promises that new citizens make in the Oath of Allegiance.

68. How can people become United States citizens?

69. What are two examples of civic participation in the United States?

70. What is one way Americans can serve their country?

71. Why is it important to pay federal taxes?

72. It is important for all men age 18 through 25 to register for the Selective Service. Name one reason why.

Part II   History

73. The colonists came to America for economic opportunity._____
   If false, write the correct answer_____

74. Africans lived in America before the Europeans arrived._____
   If false, write the correct answer_____

75. Africans were taken and sold as slaves. _____
   If false, write the correct answer_____

Multiple Choice

76. What war did the Americans fight to win independence from Britain?
   a. American Revolution   b. War of 1812
   c. Civil War   c. Vietnam War

77. Which was not a reason why the Americans declared independence from Britain.
   a. Taxation   b. Quartering
   c. Religious Freedom   d. Stamp Act

78. Who wrote the Declaration of Independence?*
   a. Thomas Jefferson   b. George Washington
   c. James Madison   d. Alexander Hamilton

79. When was the Declaration of Independence adopted?
   a. July 2, 1776   b. July 4, 1776
   c. July 4, 1796   d. July 4, 1619

Short Answer

80. The American Revolution had many important events. Name one.

81. There were 13 original states. Name five.

82. What founding document was written in 1787?

83. The Federalist Papers supported the passage of the U.S. Constitution. Name one of the writers.

84. Why were the Federalist Papers important?

85. Benjamin Franklin is famous for many things. Name one.

86. George Washington is famous for many things. Name one.

87. Thomas Jefferson is famous for many things. Name one.

88. James Madison is famous for many things. Name one.

89. Alexander Hamilton is famous for many things. Name one.

True or False

90. The United States bought Florida from France in 1803?
_____
If false, write the correct answer_____

91. The Civil War was fought by the United States in the 1800s._____
If false, write the correct answer_____

92. The War of 1812 was between the North and the South.
_____
If false, write the correct answer_____

93. The Civil War included the Battle of Gettysburg.
_____
If false, write the correct answer_____

94. Abraham Lincoln is famous for preserving the Union.
_____
If false, write the correct answer_____

Short Answer

95. What did the Emancipation Proclamation do?

96. What U.S. war ended slavery?

97. What amendment gives citizenship to all persons born in the United States?

98. When did all men get the right to vote?

99. Name one leader of the women's rights movement in the 1800s.

<u>Multiple Choice</u>

100. Name one war fought by the United States in the 1900s.
- a. Civil War
- b. World War II
- c. French and Indian War
- d. Revolutionary War

101. Why did the United States enter World War I?
- a. Impressment of sailors
- b. Pearl Harbor
- b. Germans sinking US ships
- c. Taxation

102. When did all women get the right to vote?
- a. 1918
- b. 1919
- c. 1920
- d. 1933

103. What was the longest economic recession in modern history?
- a. Great Recession
- b. The Great Migration
- c. Great Depression
- d. The Great Decline

104. When did the previous question's economic recession start?
- a. 1922
- b. 1929
- c. 1933
- d. 1941

105. Who was president during the Great Depression and World War II?
- a. Roosevelt
- b. Eisenhower
- c. Washington
- d. Truman

106. Why did the United States enter World War II?
- a. Impressment of sailors
- b. Pearl Harbor
- c. Germans sinking US ships
- c. Taxation

Short Answer

107. Dwight Eisenhower is famous for many things. Name one.

108. Who was the United States' main rival during the Cold War?

109. During the Cold War, what was the main concern of the United States?

110. Why did the United States enter the Korean War?

111. Why did the United States enter the Vietnam War?

112. What did the Civil Rights movement do?

113. Martin Luther King, Jr. is famous for many things. Name one.*

114. Why did the United States enter the Persian Gulf War?

True or False

115. Terrorists bombing the World Trade Center happened on September 11, 2001 in the United States. _____
 If false, write the correct answer_____

116. The Iraq War was after the September 11, 2001 attacks.
_____
 If false, write the correct answer_____

117. The Zulu is one American Indian tribe in the United States._____
 If false, write the correct answer_____

118.The airplane is an example of an American innovation._____
 If false, write the correct answer_____

119. New York City is the capital of the United States?_____
 If false, write the correct answer_____

120. The Statue of Liberty is located in New York City?
 If false, write the correct answer_____

121. The flag has 13 stripes for each state that seceded from the Union. _____
 If false, write the correct answer_____

Short Answer

122. Why does the flag have 50 stars?

123. What is the name of the national anthem?

124. The Nation's first motto was "E Pluribus Unum." What does that mean?

125. What is Independence Day?

126. Name three national U.S. holidays.*

127. What is Memorial Day?

128. What is Veterans Day?

Answers

1. D. Federal Republic
 Or Constitution-based federal republic
Representative democracy

2. C. (U.S.) Constitution

3. D. Include any amendments
What it does: Forms the government
Defines powers of government
Defines the parts of government
Protects the rights of the people

4. B. Only people born in America
It means: Self-government
Popular sovereignty
Consent of the governed
People should govern themselves
(Example of) social contract

5. B. Amendments
Or the amendment process

6. A. (The basic) rights of Americans
(The basic) rights of people living in the United States

7. C. Twenty-seven (27)

8. A. Declaration of Independence

9. It says America is free from British control.
It says all people are created equal.
It identifies inherent rights.
It identifies individual freedoms.

10. Equality
Liberty
Social contract
Natural rights
Limited government
Self-government

11. Declaration of Independence

12. Capitalism
Free market economy

13. Everyone must follow the law.
Leaders must obey the law.
Government must obey the law.
No one is above the law.

14. True
Declaration of Independence
Articles of Confederation
Federalist Papers
Anti-Federalist Papers
Virginia Declaration of Rights
Fundamental Orders of Connecticut
Mayflower Compact
Iroquois Great Law of Peace

15. False
So one part does not become too powerful
Checks and balances
Separation of powers

16. False
Legislative, executive, and judicial

Congress, president, and the courts

17. True
Executive branch

18. False
(U.S.) Congress
(U.S. or national) legislature
Legislative branch

19. False
Senate and House (of Representatives)

20. True
Writes laws
Declares war
Makes the federal budget

21. One hundred (100)

22. Six (6) years

23. Answers will vary. [District of Columbia residents and residents of U.S. territories should answer that D.C. (or the territory where the applicant lives) has no U.S. senators.]

24. Four hundred thirty-five (435)

25. Two (2) years

26. To more closely follow public opinion

27. Two (2)

28. Equal representation (for small states)
The Great Compromise (Connecticut Compromise)

29. Answers will vary.

30. Visit uscis.gov/citizenship/testupdates for the name of the Speaker of the House of Representatives. 2021- Pelosi

31. Citizens of their state

32. Citizens from their state

33. Citizens in their (congressional) district
Citizens in their district

34. False- Citizens from their (congressional) district elect representatives

35. True (Because of) the state's population
(Because) they have more people
(Because) some states have more people

36. False- Four (4) years

37. True- or (Because of) the 22nd Amendment
To keep the president from becoming too powerful

38. False- Visit uscis.gov/citizenship/testupdates for the name of the President of the United States. Now-Joe Biden

39. True- Visit uscis.gov/citizenship/testupdates for the name of the Vice President of the United States.

40. A. The Vice President (of the United States)

41. D. Makes Laws, that's the Legislative Branch.
The President: Signs bills into law
Vetoes bills
Enforces laws
Is Commander in Chief (of the military)

Is Chief diplomat

42. B. The President (of the United States)

43. C. The President (of the United States)

44. C. The President (of the United States)

45. C. The President (of the United States)

46. C. Senate is incorrect. The executive branch includes:
President (of the United States)
Cabinet
Federal departments and agencies

47. Advises the President (of the United States)

48. Attorney General
Secretary of Agriculture
Secretary of Commerce
Secretary of Defense
Secretary of Education
Secretary of Energy
Secretary of Health and Human Services
Secretary of Homeland Security
Secretary of Housing and Urban Development
Secretary of the Interior
Secretary of Labor
Secretary of State
Secretary of Transportation
Secretary of the Treasury
Secretary of Veterans Affairs
Vice President (of the United States)

49. It decides who is elected president.
It provides a compromise between the popular election of the
president and congressional selection.

50. Supreme Court
Federal Courts

51. Reviews laws
Explains laws
Resolves disputes (disagreements) about the law
Decides if a law goes against the (U.S.) Constitution

52. Supreme Court

53. B. Nine (9)

54. A. Five (5)

55. D. (For) life
Lifetime appointment
(Until) retirement

56. True
To be independent (of politics)
To limit outside (political) influence

57. False- John Roberts
Visit uscis.gov/citizenship/testupdates for the name of the
Chief Justice of the United States.

58. False- Federal Government does the following:
Print paper money
Mint coins
Declare war
Create an army
Make treaties
Set foreign policy

59. False- State Government does the following:
Provide schooling and education

Provide protection (police)
Provide safety (fire departments)
Give a driver's license
Approve zoning and land use

60. False (It states that the) powers not given to the federal government belong to the states or to the people.

61. Answers will vary. [District of Columbia residents should answer that D.C. does not have a governor.]

62. Answers will vary. [District of Columbia residents should answer that D.C. is not a state and does not have a capital. Residents of U.S. territories should name the capital of the territory.]

63. Citizens eighteen (18) and older (can vote).
You don't have to pay (a poll tax) to vote.
Any citizen can vote. (Women and men can vote.)
A male citizen of any race (can vote).

64. Citizens
Citizens of the United States
U.S. citizens

65. Freedom of expression
Freedom of speech
Freedom of assembly
Freedom to petition the government
Freedom of religion
The right to bear arms

66. The United States
The flag

67. Give up loyalty to other countries
Defend the (U.S.) Constitution

Obey the laws of the United States
Serve in the military (if needed)
Serve (help, do important work for) the nation (if needed)
Be loyal to the United States

68. Naturalize
Derive citizenship
Be born in the United States

69. Vote
Run for office
Join a political party
Help with a campaign
Join a civic group
Join a community group
Give an elected official your opinion (on an issue)
Contact elected officials
Support or oppose an issue or policy
Write to a newspaper

70. Vote
Pay taxes
Obey the law
Serve in the military
Run for office
Work for local, state, or federal government

71. Required by law
All people pay to fund the federal government
Required by the (U.S.) Constitution (16th Amendment)
Civic duty

72. Required by law
Civic duty
Makes the draft fair, if needed

73. True - Freedom
Political liberty
Religious freedom
Economic opportunity
Escape persecution

74. False - American Indians
Native Americans

75. True - Africans
People from Africa

76. A. American Revolution
The (American) Revolutionary War
War for (American) Independence

77. C. Religious Freedom- Correct reasons include:
High taxes
Taxation without representation
British soldiers stayed in Americans' houses (boarding, quartering)
They did not have self-government
Boston Massacre
Boston Tea Party (Tea Act)
Stamp Act
Sugar Act
Townshend Acts
Intolerable (Coercive) Acts

78. A. (Thomas) Jefferson

79. B. July 4, 1776

80. (Battle of) Bunker Hill
Declaration of Independence
Washington Crossing the Delaware (Battle of Trenton)
(Battle of) Saratoga

Valley Forge (Encampment)
(Battle of) Yorktown (British surrender at Yorktown)

81. New Hampshire
Massachusetts
Rhode Island
Connecticut
New York
New Jersey
Pennsylvania
Delaware
Maryland
Virginia
North Carolina
South Carolina
Georgia

82. (U.S.) Constitution

83. (James) Madison
(Alexander) Hamilton
(John) Jay
Publius

84. They helped people understand the (U.S.) Constitution.
They supported passing the (U.S.) Constitution.

85. Founded the first free public libraries
First Postmaster General of the United States
Helped write the Declaration of Independence
Inventor
U.S. diplomat

86. "Father of Our Country"
First president of the United States
General of the Continental Army
President of the Constitutional Convention

87. Writer of the Declaration of Independence
Third president of the United States
Doubled the size of the United States (Louisiana Purchase)
First Secretary of State
Founded the University of Virginia
Writer of the Virginia Statute on Religious Freedom

88. "Father of the Constitution"
Fourth president of the United States
President during the War of 1812
One of the writers of the Federalist Papers

89. First Secretary of the Treasury
One of the writers of the Federalist Papers
Helped establish the First Bank of the United States
Aide to General George Washington
Member of the Continental Congress

90. False- Louisiana Territory was bought in 1803
Or Louisiana

91. True- Other wars of the 1800s include
War of 1812
Mexican-American War
Civil War
Spanish-American War

92. False - The Civil War was between the North and the
South

93.True- Others events of the the Civil War include
(Battle of) Fort Sumter
Emancipation Proclamation
(Battle of) Vicksburg
(Battle of) Gettysburg
Sherman's March

(Surrender at) Appomattox
(Battle of) Antietam/Sharpsburg
Lincoln was assassinated.

94. True - Lincoln also:
Freed the slaves (Emancipation Proclamation)
Saved (or preserved) the Union
Led the United States during the Civil War
16th president of the United States
Delivered the Gettysburg Address

95. Freed the slaves
Freed slaves in the Confederacy
Freed slaves in the Confederate states
Freed slaves in most Southern states

96. The Civil War

97. 14th Amendment

98. After the Civil War
During Reconstruction
(With the) 15th Amendment
1870

99. Susan B. Anthony
Elizabeth Cady Stanton
Sojourner Truth
Harriet Tubman
Lucretia Mott
Lucy Stone

100. B. World War II - other wars of the 1900s include:
World War I
Korean War
Vietnam War

(Persian) Gulf War

101. B. Because Germany attacked U.S. (civilian) ships. Also:
To support the Allied Powers (England, France, Italy, and Russia)
To oppose the Central Powers (Germany, Austria-Hungary, the Ottoman Empire, and Bulgaria)

102. C. 1920
After World War I
(With the) 19th Amendment

103. C. Great Depression

104. B. 1929 -The Great Crash
Stock market crash of 1929

105. A. (Franklin) Roosevelt

106. B. (Bombing of) Pearl Harbor
Japanese attacked Pearl Harbor- Other Reasons the US joined:
To support the Allied Powers (England, France, and Russia)
To oppose the Axis Powers (Germany, Italy, and Japan)

107. General during World War II
President at the end of (during) the Korean War
34th president of the United States
Signed the Federal-Aid Highway Act of 1956 (Created the Interstate System)

108. Soviet Union
USSR
Russia

109. Communism
Nuclear war

110. To stop the spread of communism

111. To stop the spread of communism

112.Fought to end racial discrimination

113. Fought for civil rights
Worked for equality for all Americans
Worked to ensure that people would "not be judged by the color of their skin, but by the content of their character"

114. To force the Iraqi military from Kuwait

115. True- Terrorists attacked the United States
Terrorists took over two planes and crashed them into the World Trade Center in New York City
Terrorists took over a plane and crashed into the Pentagon in Arlington, Virginia
Terrorists took over a plane originally aimed at Washington, D.C., and crashed in a field in Pennsylvania

116. True - Other wars that took place after 9/11 include:
Global War on Terror
War in Afghanistan

117.False- Native American Tribe examples below:
Apache
Blackfeet
Cayuga
Cherokee
Cheyenne
Chippewa
Choctaw
Creek
Crow

Hopi
Huron
Inupiat
Lakota
Mohawk
Mohegan
Navajo
Oneida
Onondaga
Pueblo
Seminole
Seneca
Shawnee
Sioux
Teton
Tuscarora

118. True- Other innovations include:
Light bulb
Automobile (cars, combustible engine)
Skyscrapers
Assembly line
Landing on the moon
Integrated circuit (IC)

119. False- The capitol is Washington, D.C.

120. True- New York (Harbor)
Liberty Island [Also acceptable are New Jersey, near New
York City, and on the Hudson (River).]

121. False- The correct answer is:
(Because there were) 13 original colonies
(Because the stripes) represent the original colonies

122. (Because there is) one star for each state
(Because) each star represents a state

(Because there are) 50 states

123. The Star-Spangled Banner

124. Out of many, one
We all become one

125. A holiday to celebrate U.S. independence (from Britain)
The country's birthday

126. New Year's Day
Martin Luther King, Jr. Day
Presidents Day (Washington's Birthday)
Memorial Day
Independence Day
Labor Day
Columbus Day
Veterans Day
Thanksgiving Day
Christmas Day

127. A holiday to honor soldiers who died in military service

128. A holiday to honor people in the (U.S.) military
A holiday to honor people who have served (in the U.S. military)

Study Guide

1. What is the form of government of the United States?
Republic
Constitution-based federal republic
Representative democracy

2. What is the supreme law of the land?*
(U.S.) Constitution

3. Name one thing the U.S. Constitution does.
Forms the government
Defines powers of government
Defines the parts of government
Protects the rights of the people

4. The U.S. Constitution starts with the words "We the People."
What does "We the People" mean?

Self-government
Popular sovereignty
Consent of the governed
People should govern themselves
(Example of) social contract

5. How are changes made to the U.S. Constitution?
Amendments
The amendment process

6. What does the Bill of Rights protect?
(The basic) rights of Americans
(The basic) rights of people living in the United States

7. How many amendments does the U.S. Constitution have?*
Twenty-seven (27)

8. Why is the Declaration of Independence important?
It says America is free from British control.
It says all people are created equal.
It identifies inherent rights.
It identifies individual freedoms.

9. What founding document said the American colonies were free
from Britain?

Declaration of Independence

10. Name two important ideas from the Declaration of Independence and the U.S. Constitution.
Equality
Liberty
Social contract
Natural rights
Limited government
Self-government

11. The words "Life, Liberty, and the pursuit of Happiness" are in what founding document?

Declaration of Independence

12. What is the economic system of the United States?*
Capitalism
Free market economy

13. What is the rule of law?
Everyone must follow the law.
Leaders must obey the law.
Government must obey the law.
No one is above the law.

14. Many documents influenced the U.S. Constitution. Name one.
Declaration of Independence
Articles of Confederation
Federalist Papers
Anti-Federalist Papers
Virginia Declaration of Rights
Fundamental Orders of Connecticut
Mayflower Compact
Iroquois Great Law of Peace

15. There are three branches of government. Why?
So one part does not become too powerful
Checks and balances
Separation of powers

16. Name the three branches of government.

Legislative, executive, and judicial
Congress, president, and the courts

17. The President of the United States is in charge of which branch of government?

Executive branch

18. What part of the federal government writes laws?
(U.S.) Congress
(U.S. or national) legislature
Legislative branch

19. What are the two parts of the U.S. Congress?
Senate and House (of Representatives)

20. Name one power of the U.S. Congress.*
Writes laws
Declares war
Makes the federal budget

21. How many U.S. senators are there?
One hundred (100)

22. How long is a term for a U.S. senator?
Six (6) years

23. Who is one of your state's U.S. senators now?
Answers will vary. [District of Columbia residents and residents of U.S. territories should answer that D.C. (or the territory where the applicant lives) has no U.S. senators.]

24. How many voting members are in the House of Representatives?

Four hundred thirty-five (435)

25. How long is a term for a member of the House of Representatives?

Two (2) years

26. Why do U.S. representatives serve shorter terms than U.S. senators?

To more closely follow public opinion

27. How many senators does each state have?

Two (2)

28. Why does each state have two senators?
Equal representation (for small states)
The Great Compromise (Connecticut Compromise)

29. Name your U.S. representative.

Answers will vary. [Residents of territories with nonvoting Delegates or Resident Commissioners may provide the name of that Delegate or Commissioner. Also acceptable is any statement that the territory has no (voting) representatives in Congress.]

30. What is the name of the Speaker of the House of Representatives now?*

Visit uscis.gov/citizenship/testupdates for the name of the Speaker of the House of Representatives.

31. Who does a U.S. senator represent?
Citizens of their state

32. Who elects U.S. senators?

Citizens from their state

33. Who does a member of the House of Representatives represent?

Citizens in their (congressional) district
Citizens in their district

34. Who elects members of the House of Representatives?

Citizens from their (congressional) district

35. Some states have more representatives than other states. Why?
(Because of) the state's population
(Because) they have more people
(Because) some states have more people

36. The President of the United States is elected for how many years?*

Four (4) years

37. The President of the United States can serve only two terms. Why?

(Because of) the 22nd Amendment
To keep the president from becoming too powerful

38. What is the name of the President of the United States now?*
Visit uscis.gov/citizenship/testupdates for the name of the President of the United States.

39. What is the name of the Vice President of the United States now?*

Visit uscis.gov/citizenship/testupdates for the name of the Vice President of the United States.

40. If the president can no longer serve, who becomes president?
The Vice President (of the United States)

41. Name one power of the president.
Signs bills into law
Vetoes bills
Enforces laws
Commander in Chief (of the military)
Chief diplomat

42. Who is Commander in Chief of the U.S. military?
The President (of the United States)
43. Who signs bills to become laws?

The President (of the United States)

44. Who vetoes bills?*
The President (of the United States)

45. Who appoints federal judges?

The President (of the United States)

46. The executive branch has many parts. Name one.
President (of the United States)
Cabinet
Federal departments and agencies

47. What does the President's Cabinet do?
Advises the President (of the United States)

48. What are two Cabinet-level positions?
Attorney General
Secretary of Agriculture
Secretary of Commerce
Secretary of Defense
Secretary of Education
Secretary of Energy
Secretary of Health and Human Services
Secretary of Homeland Security
Secretary of Housing and Urban Development
Secretary of the Interior
Secretary of Labor
Secretary of State
Secretary of Transportation
Secretary of the Treasury
Secretary of Veterans Affairs
Vice President (of the United States)

49. Why is the Electoral College important?
It decides who is elected president.
It provides a compromise between the popular election of the president and congressional selection.
50. What is one part of the judicial branch?

Supreme Court
Federal Courts

51. What does the judicial branch do?
Reviews laws
Explains laws
Resolves disputes (disagreements) about the law
Decides if a law goes against the (U.S.) Constitution

52. What is the highest court in the United States?*
Supreme Court

53. How many seats are on the Supreme Court?
Nine (9)

54. How many Supreme Court justices are usually needed to decide a case?
Five (5)

55. How long do Supreme Court justices serve?
(For) life
Lifetime appointment
(Until) retirement

56. Supreme Court justices serve for life. Why?
To be independent (of politics)
To limit outside (political) influence

57. Who is the Chief Justice of the United States now?
Visit uscis.gov/citizenship/testupdates for the name of the Chief Justice of the United States.

58. Name one power that is only for the federal government.
Print paper money
Mint coins
Declare war
Create an army
Make treaties
Set foreign policy

59. Name one power that is only for the states.

Provide schooling and education
Provide protection (police)
Provide safety (fire departments)
Give a driver's license
Approve zoning and land use

60. What is the purpose of the 10th Amendment? (It states that the) powers not given to the federal government belong to the states or to the people.

61. Who is the governor of your state now?*
Answers will vary. [District of Columbia residents should answer that D.C. does not have a governor.]

62. What is the capital of your state? Answers will vary. [District of Columbia residents should answer that D.C. is not a state and does not have a capital. Residents of U.S. territories should name the capital of the territory.]

C: Rights and Responsibilities

63. There are four amendments to the U.S. Constitution about who can vote. Describe one of them.
Citizens eighteen (18) and older (can vote).
You don't have to pay (a poll tax) to vote.
Any citizen can vote. (Women and men can vote.)
A male citizen of any race (can vote).

64. Who can vote in federal elections, run for federal office, and serve on a jury in the United States?
Citizens
Citizens of the United States
U.S. citizens

65. What are three rights of everyone living in the United States?
Freedom of expression
Freedom of speech
Freedom of assembly
Freedom to petition the government
Freedom of religion
The right to bear arms

66. What do we show loyalty to when we say the Pledge of Allegiance?*
The United States
The flag

67. Name two promises that new citizens make in the Oath of Allegiance.

Give up loyalty to other countries
Defend the (U.S.) Constitution
Obey the laws of the United States
Serve in the military (if needed)
Serve (help, do important work for) the nation (if needed)
Be loyal to the United States

68. How can people become United States citizens?
Naturalize
Derive citizenship
Be born in the United States

69. What are two examples of civic participation in the United States?
Vote
Run for office
Join a political party
Help with a campaign
Join a civic group
Join a community group
Give an elected official your opinion (on an issue)
Contact elected officials
Support or oppose an issue or policy
Write to a newspaper

70. What is one way Americans can serve their country?
Vote
Pay taxes
Obey the law
Serve in the military
Run for office
Work for local, state, or federal government

71. Why is it important to pay federal taxes?
Required by law
All people pay to fund the federal government
Required by the (U.S.) Constitution (16th Amendment)
Civic duty

72. It is important for all men age 18 through 25 to register for the Selective Service. Name one reason why.
Required by law
Civic duty
Makes the draft fair, if needed

HISTORY

73. The colonists came to America for many reasons. Name one.
Freedom
Political liberty
Religious freedom
Economic opportunity
Escape persecution

74. Who lived in America before the Europeans arrived?* (Play audio (MP3, 559.78 KB))

American Indians
Native Americans

75. What group of people was taken and sold as slaves?
Africans
People from Africa

76. What war did the Americans fight to win independence from Britain?
American Revolution
The (American) Revolutionary War
War for (American) Independence

77. Name one reason why the Americans declared independence from Britain.

High taxes
Taxation without representation
British soldiers stayed in Americans' houses (boarding, quartering)
They did not have self-government
Boston Massacre
Boston Tea Party (Tea Act)
Stamp Act
Sugar Act
Townshend Acts
Intolerable (Coercive) Acts

78. Who wrote the Declaration of Independence?*
(Thomas) Jefferson

79. When was the Declaration of Independence adopted?
July 4, 1776

80. The American Revolution had many important events. Name one.
(Battle of) Bunker Hill
Declaration of Independence
Washington Crossing the Delaware (Battle of Trenton)
(Battle of) Saratoga
Valley Forge (Encampment)
(Battle of) Yorktown (British surrender at Yorktown)

81. There were 13 original states. Name five.
New Hampshire
Massachusetts
Rhode Island
Connecticut
New York
New Jersey
Pennsylvania
Delaware
Maryland
Virginia
North Carolina
South Carolina
Georgia

82. What founding document was written in 1787?
(U.S.) Constitution

83. The Federalist Papers supported the passage of the U.S. Constitution. Name one of the writers.
(James) Madison
(Alexander) Hamilton
(John) Jay
Publius

84. Why were the Federalist Papers important?
They helped people understand the (U.S.) Constitution.
They supported passing the (U.S.) Constitution.

85. Benjamin Franklin is famous for many things. Name one.
Founded the first free public libraries
First Postmaster General of the United States
Helped write the Declaration of Independence
Inventor
U.S. diplomat

86. George Washington is famous for many things. Name one.*
"Father of Our Country"
First president of the United States
General of the Continental Army
President of the Constitutional Convention

87. Thomas Jefferson is famous for many things. Name one.
Writer of the Declaration of Independence
Third president of the United States
Doubled the size of the United States (Louisiana Purchase)
First Secretary of State
Founded the University of Virginia
Writer of the Virginia Statute on Religious Freedom

88. James Madison is famous for many things. Name one.
"Father of the Constitution"
Fourth president of the United States
President during the War of 1812
One of the writers of the Federalist Papers

89. Alexander Hamilton is famous for many things. Name one.
First Secretary of the Treasury
One of the writers of the Federalist Papers
Helped establish the First Bank of the United States
Aide to General George Washington
Member of the Continental Congress

90. What territory did the United States buy from France in 1803?

Louisiana Territory
Louisiana

91. Name one war fought by the United States in the 1800s.
War of 1812
Mexican-American War
Civil War
Spanish-American War

92. Name the U.S. war between the North and the South.
The Civil War

93. The Civil War had many important events. Name one.
(Battle of) Fort Sumter
Emancipation Proclamation
(Battle of) Vicksburg
(Battle of) Gettysburg
Sherman's March
(Surrender at) Appomattox
(Battle of) Antietam/Sharpsburg
Lincoln was assassinated.

94. Abraham Lincoln is famous for many things. Name one.*
Freed the slaves (Emancipation Proclamation)
Saved (or preserved) the Union
Led the United States during the Civil War
16th president of the United States
Delivered the Gettysburg Address

95. What did the Emancipation Proclamation do?
Freed the slaves

Freed slaves in the Confederacy
Freed slaves in the Confederate states
Freed slaves in most Southern states

96. What U.S. war ended slavery?
The Civil War

97. What amendment gives citizenship to all persons born in the United States?

14th Amendment

98. When did all men get the right to vote?
After the Civil War
During Reconstruction
(With the) 15th Amendment
1870

99. Name one leader of the women's rights movement in the 1800s.

Susan B. Anthony
Elizabeth Cady Stanton
Sojourner Truth
Harriet Tubman
Lucretia Mott
Lucy Stone

C: Recent American History and Other Important Historical Information

100. Name one war fought by the United States in the 1900s.
World War I
World War II
Korean War
Vietnam War
(Persian) Gulf War

101. Why did the United States enter World War I?

Because Germany attacked U.S. (civilian) ships

To support the Allied Powers (England, France, Italy, and Russia)
To oppose the Central Powers (Germany, Austria-Hungary, the
Ottoman Empire, and Bulgaria)

102. When did all women get the right to vote?
1920
After World War I
(With the) 19th Amendment

103. What was the Great Depression?

Longest economic recession in modern history

104. When did the Great Depression start?

The Great Crash (1929)
Stock market crash of 1929

105. Who was president during the Great Depression and World War
II?

(Franklin) Roosevelt

106. Why did the United States enter World War II?

(Bombing of) Pearl Harbor
Japanese attacked Pearl Harbor
To support the Allied Powers (England, France, and Russia)
To oppose the Axis Powers (Germany, Italy, and Japan)

107. Dwight Eisenhower is famous for many things. Name one.

General during World War II
President at the end of (during) the Korean War
34th president of the United States
Signed the Federal-Aid Highway Act of 1956 (Created the Interstate
System)

108. Who was the United States' main rival during the Cold War?

Soviet Union

USSR
Russia

109. During the Cold War, what was one main concern of the United States?

Communism
Nuclear war

110. Why did the United States enter the Korean War?

To stop the spread of communism

111. Why did the United States enter the Vietnam War?

To stop the spread of communism

112. What did the civil rights movement do?

Fought to end racial discrimination

113. Martin Luther King, Jr. is famous for many things. Name one.*

Fought for civil rights
Worked for equality for all Americans
Worked to ensure that people would "not be judged by the color of their skin, but by the content of their character"

114. Why did the United States enter the Persian Gulf War?

To force the Iraqi military from Kuwait

115. What major event happened on September 11, 2001 in the United States?

Terrorists attacked the United States
Terrorists took over two planes and crashed them into the World Trade Center in New York City
Terrorists took over a plane and crashed into the Pentagon in Arlington, Virginia

Terrorists took over a plane originally aimed at Washington, D.C., and crashed in a field in Pennsylvania

116. Name one U.S. military conflict after the September 11, 2001 attacks.

(Global) War on Terror
War in Afghanistan
War in Iraq

117. Name one American Indian tribe in the United States.

Apache
Blackfeet
Cayuga
Cherokee
Cheyenne
Chippewa
Choctaw
Creek
Crow
Hopi
Huron
Inupiat
Lakota
Mohawk
Mohegan
Navajo
Oneida
Onondaga
Pueblo
Seminole
Seneca
Shawnee
Sioux
Teton
Tuscarora
For a complete list of tribes, please visit bia.gov.

118. Name one example of an American innovation.

Light bulb
Automobile (cars, internal combustion engine)
Skyscrapers
Airplane
Assembly line
Landing on the moon
Integrated circuit (IC)

SYMBOLS AND HOLIDAYS

119. What is the capital of the United States?

Washington, D.C.

120. Where is the Statue of Liberty?

New York (Harbor)
Liberty Island [Also acceptable are New Jersey, near New York City, and on the Hudson (River).]

121. Why does the flag have 13 stripes?

(Because there were) 13 original colonies
(Because the stripes) represent the original colonies

122. Why does the flag have 50 stars?

(Because there is) one star for each state
(Because) each star represents a state
(Because there are) 50 states

123. What is the name of the national anthem?

The Star-Spangled Banner

124. The Nation's first motto was "E Pluribus Unum." What does that mean?

Out of many, one
We all become one

125. What is Independence Day?

A holiday to celebrate U.S. independence (from Britain)
The country's birthday

126. Name three national U.S. holidays.

New Year's Day
Martin Luther King, Jr. Day
Presidents Day (Washington's Birthday)
Memorial Day
Independence Day
Labor Day
Columbus Day
Veterans Day
Thanksgiving Day
Christmas Day

127. What is Memorial Day?

A holiday to honor soldiers who died in military service

128. What is Veterans Day?

A holiday to honor people in the (U.S.) military
A holiday to honor people who have served (in the U.S. military)

Printed in Great Britain
by Amazon

77191689R00031